PSYCHOLOGY AND CRIME: RELEVANCE OF PSYCHOLOGY IN CRIME

VOLUME 1, ISSUE 3 OF BRAIN BOOSTER ARTICLES

OVIYA K

ISBN 979-888521691-3

Contents

Preface

"Start writing, no matter what. The water does not flow until the faucet is turned on".

-Louis L'Amour

Hundreds of students and professors are contributing their work to Brain Booster Articles, we are here to provide ample information about Law and Contemporary issues. Our aim is to provide a platform for today's generation to express their views and ideas on law and contemporary law.

Publication

This research paper is published in volume 1, issue 3 of Brain Booster Articles

CHAPTER ONE

ABSTRACT

A human brain is made up of neuron cells that release brain chemicals called neurotransmitter. These electrical signals generate wave of thousand neurons that leads to formation of thoughts. Mind is a conscious being and a product of brain activity that is made up of substances that feels, judges and perceives. The cortisol is a chemical that stimulate negative thoughts. There is saying of Gautama Buddha "The mind is everything. What you think, you become"[1]A person's subconscious mind is a powerful force that makes a person function in it's way. The psychological difficulties of a person may affect a person's mood, thinking and behavior and may cause serious disorders such as depression, bipolar disorder, anxiety, personality disorder, psychotic disorder, schizophrenia etc. these disorders may cause a person to indulge in crime and other unlawful activities. The psychology is a branch of science that studies human behavior and intentions. To handle a criminal, it is important to know his criminal intellect through which the law enforcement agencies may anticipate his next move and intention. Criminal law focuses on inducing punishments to the offender, reform, rehabilitate and deter the offenders from committing further crimes in future while the psychology helps the decision makers to pass law according to well-being of the offender (based social perceptions) and dissuade him from carrying out crimes in future. The concept of psychology in law not only helps in decision making but also formulates better treatment of offenders who are mentally ill or psychologically affected. This demonstrates the difference between the crimes that was carried out with motive and crimes carried out by a mentally affected individual this is because inducing punishments may not dissuade a mentally affected offender.

KEYWORDS: Crime, Psychology, Criminology, psychopaths, mental illness, motive, disease.

[1]Fearless Soul, https://iamfearlesssoul.com/buddha-quotes/ Accessed on November 07, Sunday at 9:27 p.m.

CHAPTER TWO

INTRODUCTION

Crimes are illegal acts carried out by an individual that is punishable under law. The word crime is derived from the Latin word called “Krimos” means “to accuse”.The term ‘psychology’ here refers to the pattern of behavior and intentions of individuals that carry out criminal acts. Criminal psychology is used to narrow down the criminal’s psyche and how the law is applied while dealing with such cases. Forensic psychologist and mental health professionals are aided to clinically evaluate the mental state of individuals that commit crimes. Psychology is a branch of science that studies the mental aspect of an individual that helps to determine the behavioral conduct of human. Psychology includes the study of conscious and unconscious state of mind through various aspect as conative, cognitive, and affective methodologies. The forensic psychologist and criminal anthropologist determine the suspects analyzing the crime scene, method of killing, weapons, injuries inflicted, investigate into psychology and other behavioral sciences. The law enforcement often relies on experts to get inside the head of the potential offender through identifying the personality type, lifestyle habits etc. In a crime, the *mens rea* of an individual plays a vital role in determining the act committed by him and criminal psychology helps to narrow down the psychological frame of mind of the culprit. In certain cases, psychology has proven culprit suffering from mental disorder that establishes such persons should be medically treated and not punished. The use of psychology in crime extends to investigate the veracity of witness as often eyewitnesses are either known to the culprit or afraid of the culprits. It also reduces false confession through adopting peace models, examination of different areas of social and legal significance and uses legal psychology rather than clinically oriented forensic psychology. Psychology also assists while pronouncing judgment as it jots downs the behavioral aspect and human mind of the culprit which ensures the proper delivery of justice.

CHAPTER THREE

BACKGROUND OF CRIMINAL PSYCHOLOGY

The psychologist in the early 20th century started to extend the scope of psychology in crime and criminal behavior. The criminal psychology was clinal in nature because the theories often focused on measuring the mental capacity of the offender. The psychologist named Goddard frequently dealt with juvenile and adult offenders whowere found to be mentally deficient.It was concluded that the primary causation of crime was the intellectual limitation and the influence of Darwinism as human defersin degree of animal brethren (some individuals are closer to animal ancestry than others).[1]The mentally deficient people are intellectually and morally less capable of adapting to modern society and resort to primitive way of meeting their needs.

Hans Toch published the first criminal psychologybook (KriminalPsychologie) in the year 1897, which details his observation on offenders, witnesses, jurors and judges. However, itconfidesonly little on psychological research.[2]

Hans J. Eysenck, a British psychologist in crime and personality published in the year 1964developed the first theoretical statements on criminal psychology focusing on biological factors including personality, characteristics of extroversion and introversion, learning experience obtained from an individual's social environment. However, this was replaced by the popular developmental approach proposed by Edwin Megargee (1966) laid down the under-controlled and over-controlled personalities and their relationship accompanied by violence. Followed by Toch (1969)on violent men. Leonardo Berkowitz (1962), Albert Bandura (1973), Bandura and Walters (1959) and Robert Baron (1977) discussed on aggression and violence. And later psychiatrist Hervey Cleckley (1941/

1964) emphasized on psychopaths which became a theory to build various research by Canadian psychologist Robert Hare (1970), now the psychopathy continues to be strong field of research for criminal behavior till date.[3]

[1]Criminal Justice, http://criminal-justice.iresearchnet.com/forensic-psychology/history-of-forensic-psychology/criminal-psychology/Accessed on November 08, Monday at 6.30 p.m.

[2]Criminal Justice, http://criminal-justice.iresearchnet.com/forensic-psychology/history-of-forensic-psychology/criminal-psychology/ Accessed on November 08, Monday at 6.30 p.m.

[3]Criminal Justice, http://criminal-justice.iresearchnet.com/forensic-psychology/history-of-forensic-psychology/criminal-psychology/ Accessed on November 08, Monday at 6.30 p.m.

CHAPTER FOUR

CRIME: TYPES, OFFENDERS AND HUMAN NATURE

The term 'crime' means any act committed with a malicious intention by an individual which is punishable under law.Any act to constitute as a crime must be carried out with intention by the perpetrator and shall generally cause disturbance to public peace. In a crime, *mens rea* is important factor to determine the offence. Criminal psychology provides more than a criminal's psyche and extends to establish the legal psychology and how the law is applied. While dealing with the criminals the psychologist often examines the complex mix of personality, lifestyle, genetics, life circumstances and environmental factors. They take up investigation with the individuals that have committed crimes or those that are victims of crimes, this is done to understand and explore how criminals choose victims. They examine and jot down what the law enforcements and policy makers can do to prevent occurrence of such crimes in future. The inquisition of why an individual commit crime is often the root of criminal psychology. The criminal psychology is that the branch of study that deals with the intentions and behavior of person who plan and perform criminal activities. The criminal psychology does more than determining a criminal's psyche. It establishes the connection between the mindset of the criminal, intention, consciousness while committing the crime and law, which in order renders way to fair judgment.

Why do people commit crime?

The question of why people commit crimes and what could possibly deter a person from committing offence in the future is the core of psychologist and law enforcement officers. The criminal psychologist, forensic psychologist and criminal anthropologist often rely on undertaking research of a criminal's lifestyle, environment, genetics, life circumstances, personality etc. while determining the intention and mindset of the criminal. Some individuals commit crime out of certain necessity while others are driven by anger, manipulative personality, psychopathic tendencies, or rejection of authority etc. There are several instances during which the psychosis substance/drug abuse or severe maniac depression can influence aprivate being to commit crime or break the law. Though all mentally ill people are prone to commit crime is a myth.

However, the question of why people commit crimes and what factors influence a person to indulge in criminal activities can be broadly explained through four theories of crime:

Biological theories of crime:

The biological theory of crimes includes genetics,brain chemistry, brain structure and anatomy. The genetics is seen as a key factor to commission of crime. This theory assumes that some people are born criminals and these individual psychologically differ from the non-criminals. The part of brain related to emotion is namedAmygdala. Any damage to amygdala can have an impact of criminal behavior which alleviates fear and conditioning response and thus punishmentdoes not deter an individual from committing crime.

Serotonin is a neurotransmitter in brain that affects the mood of an individual which can also causes an individual to indulge in criminal activity while the testosterone is a male hormone which is linked with level of aggression within the conduct of an individual. These genetic factors lead a being to enjoy criminality.

The Hippocampus is component of brain where the memories are stored, when any damage occurs to the present area, an individual loses his memory, which ultimately result the person to repeat an equivalent offence or crime that he was punished without being conscious of earlier times.

The Frontal Cortex/frontal area is that front part of brain which involves in self-control and other related functions.

The Phineas cage: This case is concerningbrain damage resulting to vary in self-control of person named Phineas Cage. In the year 1848, Phineas Cage was a railroad worker overseeing the laying of explosives in a hole and tapping it down with tamping iron with 3'8 long and 1.5 in diameter, the spark ignited the explosive and the tamping iron landed onto his left cheek and out through frontal area, however, Phineas survived the accident. But after his full recovery he was no longer a mild mannered and conscientious, he became impatient, impulsive and abusive. The damage to the frontal area caused the change in Phineas.[1]

Socialization theory of crime:

The socialization theory in crime includesstrain theory, social learning theory, control theory, routine activity theory andvarious social factors that influence an individual to commit crimes which incorporates behavior learnt or adapted by an individual or child modeling the elders, environmental factors etc. Humans are capable of developing, learning and adapting to certain models, movements, behavior that are influential and attractive to them.

The routine activity theory connected with social learning theory is based on motivation, attractive target andlack of capable guardian. The offender's everyday routine may influence commission of crimes. Instances where there is a motivated offender who meets an attractive target without a guardian.

The strain theory states that an individual indulges in criminal activities due to lot of stress, negativity, anxiety they experience. These individuals indulge in criminal activities to scale back their strain. The stress may arise out of poverty, social circumstances, breakage of family etc.

However, unlike the opposite theories control theory is seeks to establish that an individual may commit crime or indulge in unlawful activities when the desires of the person can easily be fulfilled through unlawful means compared to legal channels.

Behavioral theory of crime

A human behavior is learned through observation, adaption and learning experience. A person's behavior may be elicited through rewards and extinguished by negative reactions and punishments. An individual develops aggression, violence through learned process or behavior modeling from observing family interactions, environmental experience and mass media.

The situational choice theory focuses on the circumstances which influenced the person to commit a crime. Under this theory an individual commits crime out of circumstances or situational constrains and opportunities. The individual's behavior is based on the given situation.

Economic theory of crime

The crimes under this theory are done with a motive of economic gain. This type of crime is carried out by an individual or group of individualsin an illegal manner to gain financial returns. An individual may commit crime due to poverty, lack of education, inequality among the rich and the poor in same community etc.

How does a perpetrator choose his victim?

The criminals choose victims based on how the individual look or move. The criminals often choose victims when the person appears noticeably different from those around them or were moving in distracted or unusual way.

The finding of the psychological and psychiatric mechanism has a significant influence upon the legal system in the beginning of 20th century. These changes include deinstitutionalization of mentally ill that strive for the development of advanced psychiatric medications, understanding the causes and potential treatments for mental disorder. The legal professions including lawyers, police officers, judge's psychologist could assess the defendant's state of mind and shall provide treatment if necessary. The psychology and law examine the human behavior. However, the first seeks to understand and the latter seeks to regulate where such is necessary. These studies help the policymakers to write laws that are in the interest of public.

The concept of crime seems to have been changing with changes in the social conditions and evolutionary stages of human society. Every human society have certain norms, conduct of behavior and customs considered by its members to be socially well-being and a healthy development. When such conducive is broken by an act of anti-social, immoral, and sinful behavior forbidden by law is a crime. Crimes can be classified on basis of motive of the offender while committing such acts. They are as follows:

- Predatory crimes
- Violent crimes
- Inchoate crimes
- Hate crime
- Crime without victim
- Organized crime
- White collar crime
- Cyber crime
- Sexual offences

A person is said to have committed crime when the gravity of harm caused by the misconduct of a person affects the society than an individual. All immoral activities do not constitute a crime. Crimes are immoral and illegal activities carried out by the perpetrator which is punishable under the existing penal law. Any act to constitute a crime must be carried out with the following elements:

- External consequences
- Harm must be specifically outlawed
- Actus Reus
- *Mens-rea*
- Prohibited act
- Relation between the act and injury
- Punishment

Every individual has different interest, likings, dislikes, opinion and intellect. One person's definition of moral attitude may not be another person's conducive of moral act. One person's ability to distinguish between the right and wrongful act may not be another's ability. Crimes committed by every person have certain motive, necessity or a backstory which makes them anoffender. The theories of human nature and the criminality can be classified as conformity perspective, non-conformity perspective, neutral being.

The conformity perspective according to Merton R. K lays down those humans are fundamentally good people and are strongly influenced by values and attitudes of the society. while the non-conformist perspective theory assumes that humans are in disciplined creatures prone to commit crime. The third perspective states humans are neutral being by birth and they learn their beliefs, behavior, tendencies and model from their social environment. An individual may commit crime out of anger, poverty, low self-esteem, drug abuse which turns them into an offender. The causation of crime discerns a difference between each type of offender which can be classified based on their necessity, motive and crime frequency:

1. Habitual criminal
2. Moralistic criminal
3. Psychopathic criminal
4. Institutional criminal or white-collar criminal
5. Situational or occasional criminal
6. Professional criminal
7. Organized criminals
8. Juvenile delinquents

[1]Annerivendell, Psychology Of Crime: Why Do People Become Criminals, Owlcation, https://owlcation.com/social-sciences/Psychology-of-Crime-Why-do-people-become-criminals Accessed on November 08, Monday at 7.30 p.m.

CHAPTER FIVE

HEREDITY AND CRIME

Every criminologist has different views on causation of criminal offence or crime. Often criminologist rely and support on the endogenous theory of criminality found in the bio-physical consideration and social factors of the criminals. It seeks to examine the nature of the criminals rather than his personality. criminologist however conclude that hereditary influences have little effect on the individual's criminality which can be further pointed out through certain clans and tribes like gypsies in the western Europe usually indulge in criminality for generations. The Kanjars and Lohars in Rajasthan state of India and Baluchis are few nomadic tribes who habitually pursue criminal activities and traits as a mode of life. In certain cases, the wrongful environment and family also influence an individual to indulge in criminal acts. However, in the studies carried out by Goring Healy, Glueck and Scheldon stated that the co-relation between heredity as a factor of crime causation is difficult to establish.[1]

[1]Prof. N. V. Paranjape, Criminology, Penology Victimology, 61-62 (Central Law Publications 2018)

CHAPTER SIX

HOW DOES MENTAL DISORDER IMPACT CRIMINALITY?

The term 'mental disorder' means abnormality. A state of confusion or unstable mind or recurring instances of lunacy. In a study conducted by Coid in the year 1940 indicated a low rate of co-relation between the mental disorder and criminality among criminals. However, it suggests that psychological problems were common among criminals. Prisoners were very naïve in developing mental health problems since prison is the place where criminals must reside for a long period and usually in isolation.[1] Especially, criminals that have committed grave offences such as sexual assaults, murder, robbery must stay in prison for longer period. The common psychiatric issues or disorders that criminals suffer are depression, anxiety, psychoses, personality disorder, substance misuse leading to suicidal risk. (Baillargeon et al,2009 and Fazel et al, 2008) the alienation from family and society, delay in legal proceedings may develop hopelessness which is a prominent cause that increases stress and other mental health related problems. Prisoners also face other problems that deteriorate the psychological wellbeing such as problem of overcrowding, unhygienic cell environment, group clashes and conflicts inside the prison, solitary confinement, past history on treatment of mental disorder, diagnosis of schizophrenia.[2] After the release of the criminals, they are often stigmatized as 'offender' by the societies while some adapt to the circumstances and others start feeling guilty and develop aggression, suicidal behavior, stress, depression, anxiety, and other psychiatric problems. The research conducted by Castellano and Soderstrom, 1997 have shown that prisoners show an elevated anxiety and depression compared to normal population. In the study conducted by the Global Journal of Human-Social Science in the year 2015 stated that the rapist has revealed more occurrence of anxiety symptoms than murderers. Rapist with population of 37.5% have had anxiety (12.5% mild, 15.6% moderate and 9.4% severe anxiety) while murderer group of 20% have had 2.5% mild, 12.5% moderate and 5.0% severe anxiety.[3]

In various faces there are number of factors that is commonly shared among the criminals and psychiatric patients as demographic variables like age, socio-economic status, race. And patients with personality disorder share a common factor with criminals usually as a young men, poorly educated, unemployment, disorganized home environment, deprived upbringing, or no parental guidance. In other cases, poverty, lack of social support, exposure to severe trauma, child sexual abuse causes psychiatric illness in later stage that leads to adverse effect of criminality or antisocial personality. however, not all persons with mental illness are prone to commit crimes. In situations mental illness patient may commit crimes when they are paranoid, deluded, left undiagnosed or untreated, command hallucinations etc.

REPEAT OFFENDER

Repeat offender is an individual who commit the same offence again after being prosecuted and convicted for previous time. Recidivism is a tendency of a criminal to commit the same offence again.An individual may reoffend out of various circumstances such as mental illness, unemployment, drug and alcohol addiction. Most of the offenders in the prison do not get proper treatment and after their release they may lack proper therapy and medication, necessary coping skills etc. while some individual may repeat the same offence due to unemployment, poverty, lack of money to meet their needs. This is because the employment opportunity is scarce and the convicted personalities are not favorably looked upon in jobs and society and most of the times people with previous conviction do not get jobs easily. This stigmatization in society may crumble the self-confidence of an individual leading the person to suffer depression and anxiety. Depression is common among the individuals after their release because some may find difficulty in adjusting to the society. Prisoners who have spent their adulthood and those that do not have family or place to go after their release may have no choice but to go back. While Offenders with substance abuse may after their release seek the addiction habits and to fund their dependence on drug, they tend to commit crimes.

SUBSTANCE ABUSE

The term substance abuse means harmful or hazardous use of psychoactive substances, Alcohol, drugs which causes severe health and social problems for individuals who consume it, as well as their families and communities. The diagnosis of the substances abuse puts an individual at the risk of violence more than any other form of mental illness.[4]

JUVENILE DELIQUENCY:

The term delinquency is abnormality in which a person deviates from course of normal social life while juvenile means a person who is a minor. The juvenile delinquency is when a minor exhibits behavior that is dangerous to the society. A child or a minor may develop certain behavioral traits that are harmful in nature due to various factors such as bad company, mental conflicts, broken family, environmental situation, love of adventure, running away from home etc.

PSYCHOPATH BEHAVIOR

A person's personality is controlled by unconscious mental process. Psychopathy also known as the antisocial personality disorder (ASPD or APD) is psychological personality disorder in which an individual lacks emotion and empathy and display a specific temperament such as lack of fear, lack of inhibition, stimulus seeking behavior, psychological idiosyncrasies like reduced physical response to negative stimuli, threat of pain and punishment. Hare and associates influenced by Cleckley's observations laid down twenty-two traits under the 'Psychopathy Checklist' (PCL) which was grouped into two factors namely narcissistic personality and antisocial behavior.

Hare's Psychopathy Checklist further enhanced the psychopathy personality traits as:

- Lack of remorse or empathy,
- Hallow emotions,
- Manipulativeness,
- Lying,
- Egocentricity,
- Glibness,
- Low frustration tolerance,
- Episodic relationship,
- Parasitic lifestyle,
- The persistent violation of social norms,

- Need for stimulation and criminal versatility,
- Pathological lying,
- Failure to accept responsibility for own actions,
- Lack of realistic and long-term goals
- Superficial charm.[5]

According to research, the psychopathy emerges early in life and persists to middle age. In certain instances, the prototypical psychopaths are responsible for certain heinous crimes. Psychopaths are intelligent people; they hold an elite position in society and their intention is to harm anyone in a heinous manner. They hold pure sadistic feeling and enjoy watching others in pain. Psychopaths are deceitful and fraudulent with their identity and it is difficult to identify them in society.

In India, there have been numerous crimes reported on serial killings, mental illness, incest, and other sexual and violent crimes but there are none regarding the psychopath. But if we investigate these reported cases, various incidents indicate instances of psychopathic tendencies of the offender. The Thug Behram of Thugee clan, one of the world's most prolific killers reportedly killed more than 900 people with ceremonial cloth and was executed in the year 1840 by hanging.[6]

[1]Neelu Sharma, Om Prakash, Dr. K.S Sengar, Dr. A.R. Singh, A Study of Mental Health Problems in Criminals in Terms of Depression, Anxiety and Stress, Global Journal of Human-Social Science Research, 3-6, 2015.

[2]*Ibid* 6

[3]*Ibid* 6

[4]Substance Abuse, National Health Portal of India, https://www.nhp.gov.in/disease/non-communicable-disease/substance-abuse Accessed on November 10, Wednesday at 5:45 p.m.

[5]The Psychopathy Checklist-Revised (PCL-R), http://www.clintools.com/victims/resources/assessment/personality/psychopathy_checklist.html Accessed on November 10, Wednesday at 5:59 p.m.

[6]Priya Sepaha, Psychopaths: An Unrevealed Area in Indian Judicial System,http://docs.manupatra.in/newsline/articles/Upload/1FCAC641-A31A-4A18-8F02-7BFAFE977E34.pdf Accessed on November 10, Wednesday at 7:00 p.m.

CHAPTER SEVEN

RELEVANT CASES

In 1989, The Stoneman, a name given by English language print media of Kolkata to a serial killer who was charged with 13 murders in six months (the first in June of same year) however, it was unable to be established whether these crimes were a handiwork of an individual or group of persons. Till date there is no clue to whether these crimes are copycat murders, and no one is sentenced for the offence, this case still remains one of the greatest unsolved mysteries.[1]

The Beer Man, name given to suspected serial killer who reportedly murdered 7 people between October 2006 to January 2007 in south Mumbai, India. The killer left beer bottles beside each body that was the only link between the deaths.[2]

Auto Shankar, nickname of serial killer who was found guilty of 6 murders along with his gang. The bodies of the victims were either buried inside residential houses or burnt. The crime was committed over a period of 2 years from 1988-1989.[3]

In the Joshi-Abhyanker murder case, the accused Rajendra Jakkal, Dilip Dhyanoba Sutar, Shantaram Kanhoji Jagtap and Munawar Harun Shah were commercial art student of Abhinav Kala Mahavidyalaya in the Pune state of India. They allegedly committed 10 murders between the year of January 1976 and March 1977 and had acquired reputation of bad conduct in their college campus. They have been frequently involved in robbery and drinking. The offenders were hanged to death on 27 November 1983.[4]

Raman Raghav a psychopathic serial killer was diagnosed with schizophrenia after his arrest in the city of Mumbai in mid-1960s Raman Ragav's sentence was reduced to life imprisonment due to the underlining disorder and was found incurably mentally ill.[5]

Charles Sobhraj was a high-profile criminal from India, also known as 'Bikini Killer' because of few of his victims' bodies were found wearing bikini. He allegedly killed 12 by strangulation and poisoning. Charles Sobhraj was a high profiler killer because of his high-society lifestyle and constant quest for adventure.[6]

Dandupalya Krishna was the leader of dandupalya gang which operated across Karnataka and Andhra Pradesh state of India between August 1995 to October 1999. They killed 42 people and more than 100 unofficial figures have been cited. They used crowbar and other weapons to murder their victims. All the members of the gang were convicted and sentenced to capital punishment in 1999 and with fine of Rs. 30,000 each.[7]

Darbara Singh was arrested by the police in October 2004 when 23 children aged below 10 were gone missing in various parts of Punjab. Out of which 6 children were recovered by the police while Darbara confessed that he had killed 17 children (15 girls and 2 boys) out of rage. He confessed he had tried to rape and sodomise his victims after killing them. The court sentenced capital punishment for Darbara Singh.[8]

All the above-mentioned cases specify the disease of psychopathy of the accused person. Often psychopathy is confused with crimes committed with *mens rea* which cannot be collectively measured for considering judgements and trials. Since the *mens rea* behind all criminal activities differ and distinct with each crime. but however, the offences committed by the psychopath often is motive-less or simply pure pleasure.

The psychopathy is often confused with serial killing, rape, incest, sociopathy and other sexual and violent crimes, but they cannot be collectively measured together since the motive in psychopathy crimes are absent in most cases and carried out of joy/disease.

However, if we investigate the cases of rape, sodomy, serial killing child molestation, incest may have been committed out of aggression, obsession, revenge, pleasure, fun, lust. But when such crimes are committed out of psychopathy tendency, it is a disease. It differs from crimes committed with motive or by a mentally ill individual.

Crimes committed with motive

An individual may commit crime when the outcome of such criminal acts overweighs the consequences of breaking a law. A wrongful act can amount to crime in instances where the individual has carried out such an act with a motive or guilty mind (*mens rea*). The intention of a person while committing a wrong determines the severity of the act, whether such acts can be treated as a crime or mere wrongful act. A wrong may or may not be forbidden by law but any act that is forbidden and sanctioned by law amounts to crime. Unlike psychopaths, people who commit crimes with motive are conscious of the punishments and consequences for breaking the law while psychopaths are individuals that lack remorse, human emotion and does not fear punishments, they commit crimes out of their psychopath tendencies/disease.

Ways to deal with psychopaths under legal methodology

In the Nithari rape case, Surendra Koli v. State of Uttar Pradesh and Ors[9] the accused that mercilessly killed and eaten the flesh of children confessed that "I still have an urge to kill" he also involved in abduction, rape and murdering a woman and later mutilated the corpse of his victims. The victim was beheaded and the head along with the garments were thrown in drain behind Pandher's residence. The CBI court observed this as 'rarest of rare' and sentenced capital punishment to the offender which was six years after the conviction reduced to life imprisonment by Allahabad High Court.

Punishments are awarded to induce fear in the minds of offenders which will restrain him from committing such crimes in future but in case of psychopaths, the offender himself is fearless and unconcerned about the severity of the punishments, and the crimes committed by such person is result of his psychopath tendencies or mental illness and not because of a guilty mind or motive (*mens rea*). In these cases, leveling up the punishments to prevent the wrongdoer from committing such crimes in future do not solve the problem. Psychopaths are devoid of human emotion, and they lack remorse or fear of punishment.

[1]Crimes From The East, https://www.podpage.com/crimes-from-the-east/the-stoneman-serial-murders/ Accessed on November 10, Wednesday at 7:25 p.m.

[2]The Indian Express, http://archive.indianexpress.com/news/beer-man-acquitted-in-murder-case/518416/ Accessed on November 10, Wednesday at 7:35 p.m.

[3]Gauri Shankar And Ors. V. State of Tamil Nadu, 1994 CriLJ 3071

[4]Munawar Harun Shah and Ors. V. State of Maharashtra, AIR 1983 SC 585

[5]State of Maharashtra v. Sindhi Raman, 1975 AIR 1665

[6]Charles Sobhraj V. State, 1996 IIAD Delhi 550

[7]Dandupalya Krishna V. State of Karnataka, Criminal Appeal No.538/2014

[8]The State of Punjab Prosecutor V. Darbara Singh, Criminal Appeal No. 138-DB of 2008

[9]Criminal Appeal No(s). 2227 of 2010

CHAPTER EIGHT

LEGAL PROVISION

- Section 84 of Indian Penal Code, 1860 deals with 'act of person of unsound mind' as defense. It states that any act carried out by an individual which is done out of unsoundness of mind or was incapable of knowing the nature of the act or was unsoundness of mind while doing an act that is either wrong or contrary to law.
- However, section 328 of the Code of Criminal Procedure, 1973 deals with procedure in case of accused person being lunatic. It deals with instances where the person against whom the inquiry is being held is lunatic or unsoundness of mind. Nonetheless these provisions remain insufficient in cases of partial delusions, irresistible impulse and impulsive behavior of psychopaths.
- In India, offenders suffering from high grade of mental illness are brought into rehabilitation centers on grounds of insanity that makes them a patient more than as an offender and are treated pitifully.

CHAPTER NINE

CRIMINAL PSYCHOLOGY AND ROLE OF CRIMINAL PSYCHOLOGIST:

The criminal psychologist studies the intentions, mental stability, reactions, views and thoughts of criminals while committing a crime and after commission of crime. The criminal psychologist and the criminal anthropologist are interrelated and helps in narrowing down the causation of a crime. The criminal psychologist is often called to court to study the mind of offender and to deal with their criminal behavior.

They extend assistance in investigation of crime, examining the crime scene photographs, interview the suspect, formulating a hypothesis on the next step of the offender. They examine the pattern of behavior and determine whether the offender is competent for trial and whether such person can be put back into the society.

The question of insanity, sanity or criminal responsibilityof a person can be retorted with the offender'sstate of mind, whether such person is capable of understanding the right and wrongful acts. The defense of insanity is difficult to be proved but if the offender is declared insane, then he shall be sent for psychiatric hospital.

These legal psychologist in the legal proceedings deal with social and cognitive principles and how they are applied in usage. They are often seen in various roles that influences decision-making in the court. They are the ones that make decisions on the offenders after determining whether they are threat to the society or competent for trial.

Relevance of legal psychology in legal proceedings

- **Advisory, Academic and Research**: The legal psychologist provides advices to the decision makers about the psychological issues in the case. They conduct legal researches on new topics that have not been popularized and work as a guide to legal representatives.
- **Trial consulting, Policy making and legislative guidance**: The trial consultants help assisting in a particular case with their expertise. Their work is based on empirical research and establish policies based on the empirical research. They also assist in the time of crisis and help national and state lawmakers.
- **Amicus briefs and expert witness**: The legal psychologists provide opinion based on scientific statistics and backup. They assist in testifying the witness's competency.
- **Offender profiling**: The criminal psychologist studies the thoughts and behavior of criminals through which a person's personality, emotions, mental characteristics and his response to the crime can be ascertained. This is a process that involves studying and analyzing the crime scene and behavioral aspects of a perpetrator in a crime scene where there is an exhibition of psychopathology.The criminal investigative analyst is experienced and are trained law enforcement officers that deal with establishing thecharacteristics of a criminal which can be ascertained through certain preparations or movements in the crime scene as follows:

1. Amount of planning involved in commission of crime.
2. Aggregate control used by the perpetrator in crime scene.
3. Escalation of emotion.
4. Risk level of perpetrator and victim.
5. Whether the crime scene was organized or disorganized.

- **Rapport maintaining**: The criminal psychologist often uses this technique to ascertain the person's personality and mental characteristics. Rapport is a condition in which two individuals are able to connect and communicate with each other. Through this method the criminologist tries to cultivate confidence in the mind of the offender and maintains an effective communication to grasp the thoughts of offender without any pressure, through eye contact, mutual attention and mirroring body postures etc. they understand the small gestures and motions (sweating, nervousness, enlarged pupil etc.) of the offender and discover the criminal's mind.

CHAPTER TEN

CRIMINAL ANTHROPOLOGY

According to Darwinism, humans evolved from animals and certain individual may possess animal behavior compared to others or simply certain individual are closer to animal ancestry than others and may exhibit characteristics that may defer from non-criminals. They may not be capable of controlling their urge to commit crimes. The criminal anthropology is a branch of sociology that focus on investigating into crime scientifically. It is a study relating to the origin, cause and determines the possible proportion of responsibility that falls on society and the offender.

CRITICISM OF CONCEPT OF PSYCHOLOGY IN LAW

The psychology is a branch of science that studies a human conduct and behavior. This study may not be certain but when such study is to be applied in the usage of law, it requires certainty. The psychology defenses are often used for limited scope and can be seen widely in criminal law. these theories and amicus brief are only used to support the personal belief of the psychologist due to lack of training.

AUTHOR'S CRITIC

Psychology is a branch of science and the usage of scientific explanation in law pertaining to how an individual defer from non-criminals and how a person is prone to indulge in criminal activities may help the law makers to enact laws and pass decisions considering the psychological issues in a case. The law makers while considering the psychological difficulties and issues of the offender shall pass decisions for well-being of the offender and to deter him from committing crimes in future. Punishments may not always deter a person from committing a crime because punishing an offender who is a mentally illor psychologically affected may not dissuade him from committing crimes. This is because the person is neither in a stable state of mind to understand the consequences nor has any human emotion or fear of being punished. Psychology and crime are interrelated and is a strong field for research. However, often the psychological explanations to a problem may not always be useful in practical usage.

CHAPTER ELEVEN

CONCLUSION

Psychology studies the mental characteristics of an individual that helps in determining the human behavior of a person. The usage of psychology in crime and criminal investigation and analysis helps the investigative officers to narrow down the behavioral characteristics, movement and mental stability of the offender or suspect. This studies the conscious and unconscious state of mind. The law enforcement agencies often rely on the forensic psychologist, criminal anthropologist while identifying the potential culprit by way of analyzing the life style, movement, preparation (organized or unorganized), personality type, weapon and method of execution of crime and habits etc. considering the psychological difficulties in the case may pave way to decision makers and law enforcement agencies in determining the *Mens rea* of a person and their psychological frame of mind. The findings of psychology in crime have often proven that criminals are individual that suffer mentally and thus they must be treated and not punished. However, crimes committed with *Mens rea* is confused with psychopathy crimes, while individuals that commit crimes out of a motive and targeted victim are conscious of consequences for breaking the law. Crimes carried out with motive differ from crimes committed by person out of psychopathy tendencies/disease. Psychology has established that crimes committed in course of psychopathy or crimes that exhibit psychopathic behavior of the offender are often motiveless and carried out of disease. They lack human emotion and fear of punishment. Imposing punishment to a mentally ill and psychologically affected person will not dissuade them from committing further crimes in future. Over time, the understanding of psychology has helped to bring significant changes in the criminal justice system and is an eye-opener to treat criminals who are mentally ill or psychologically affected according to the pictures of human preferences and perceptions.

Printed by Libri Plureos GmbH in Hamburg,
Germany